Colors All Around

M000236301

By Jim Lobes
Illustrated by Al Lorenz

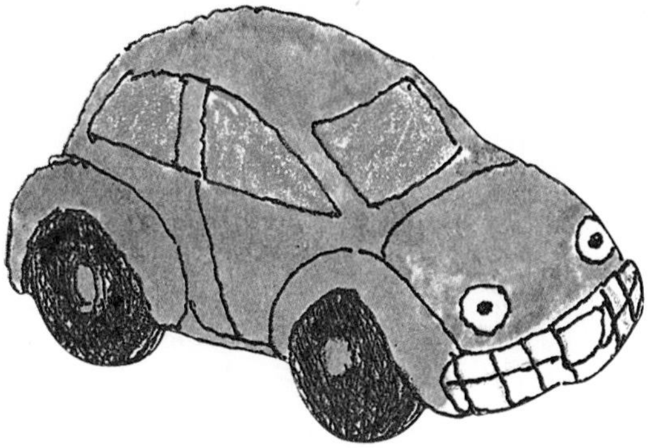

Target Skill Color Recognition

Scott Foresman
is an imprint of
PEARSON

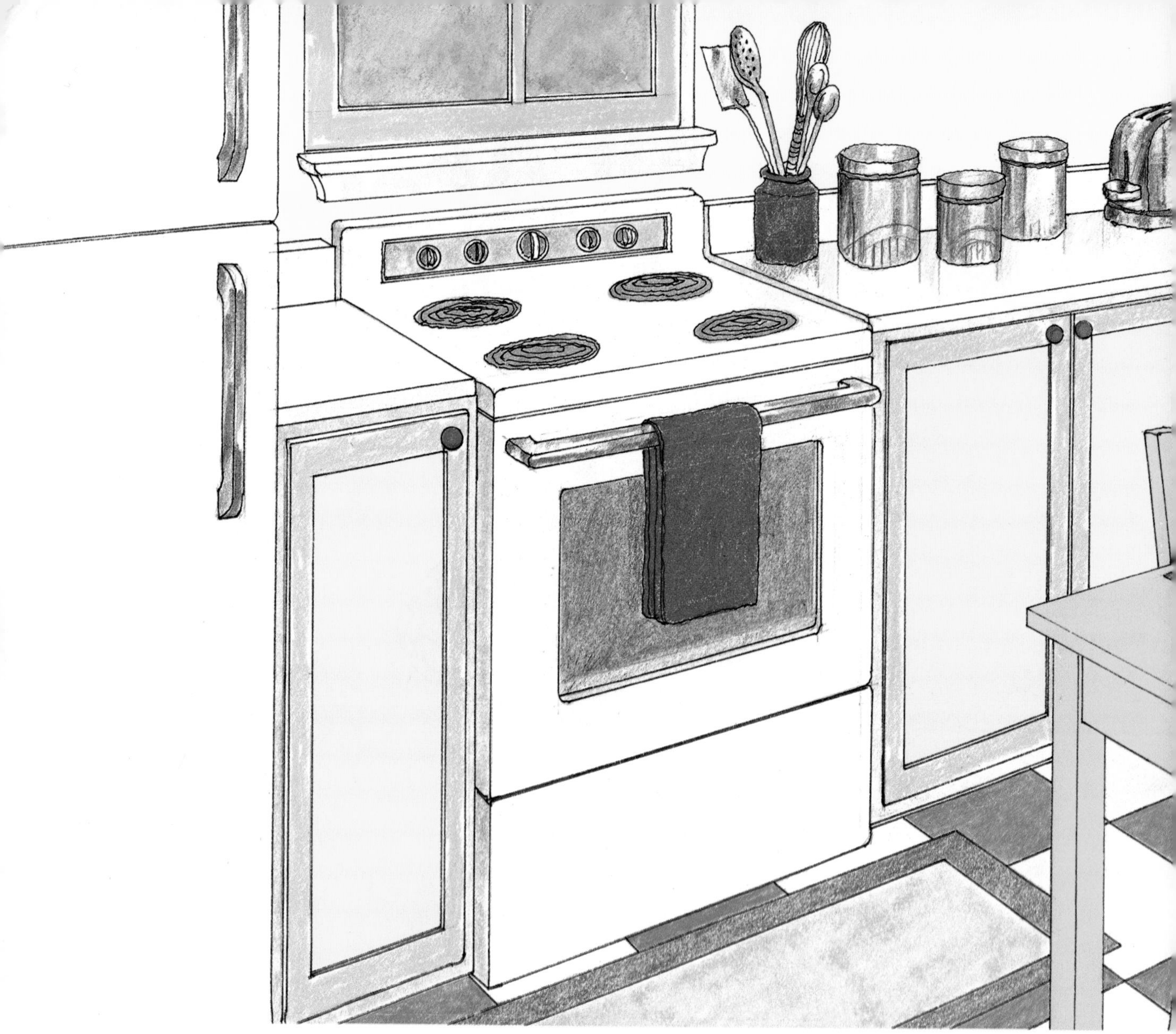

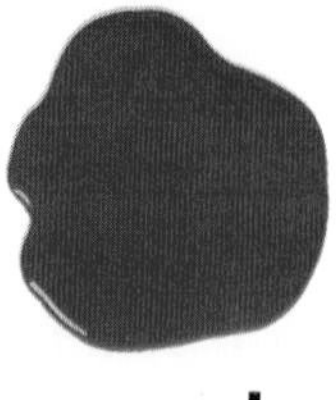

red

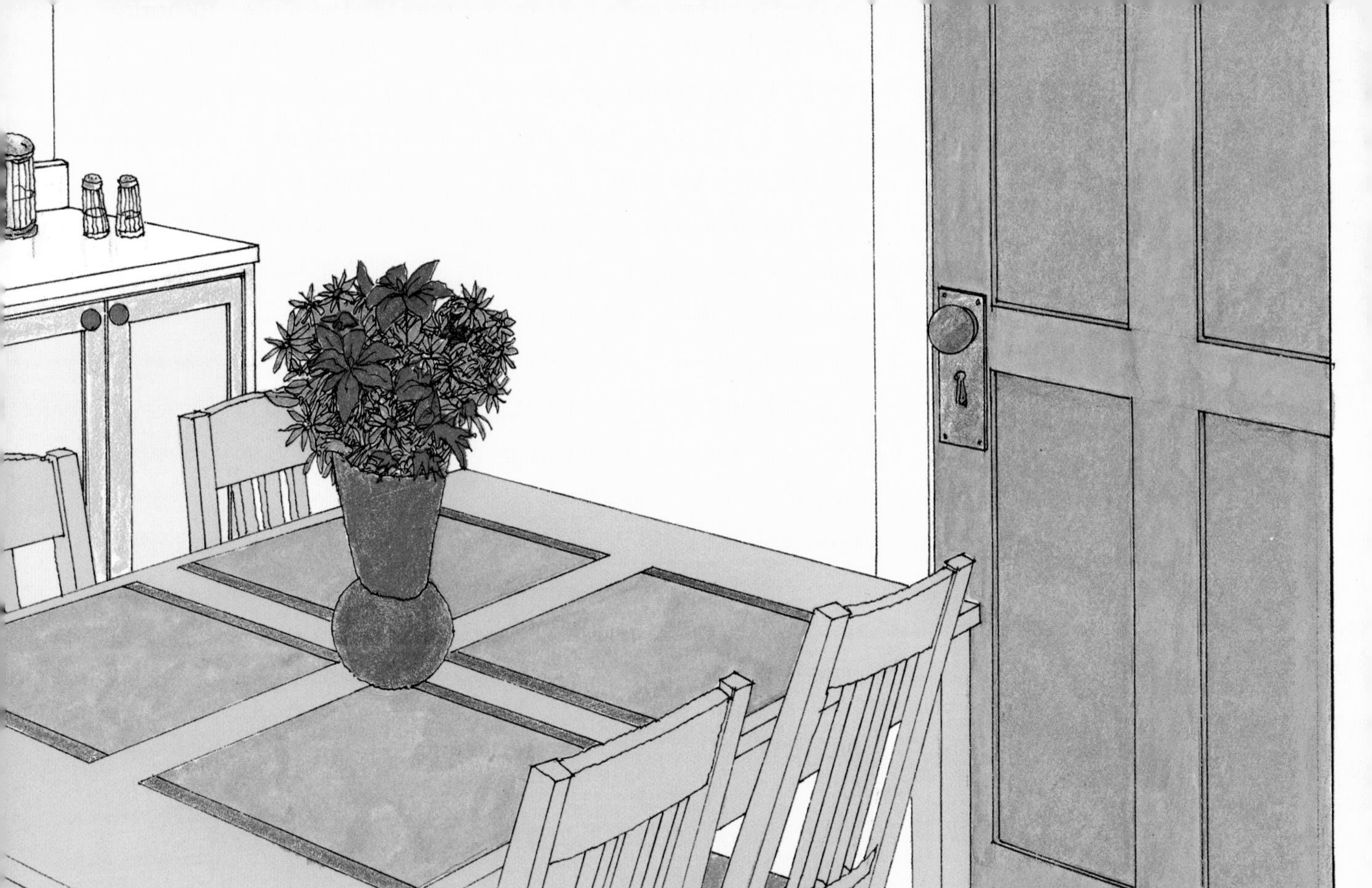

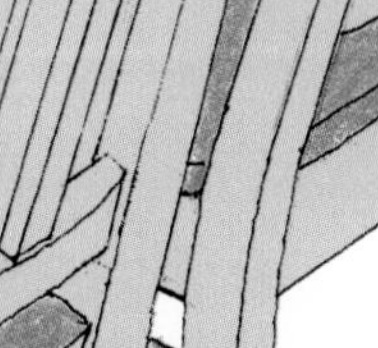

blue

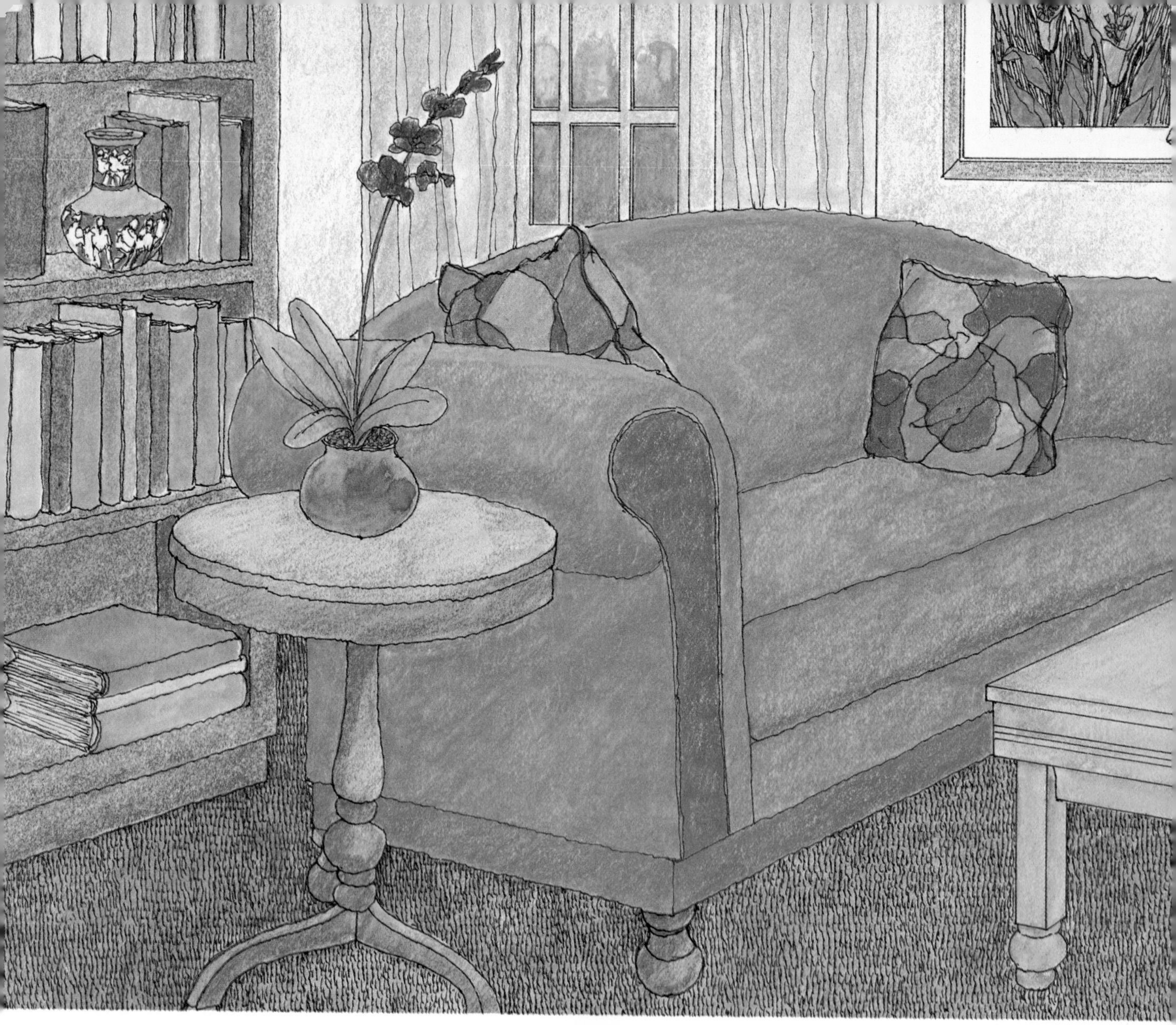

yellow

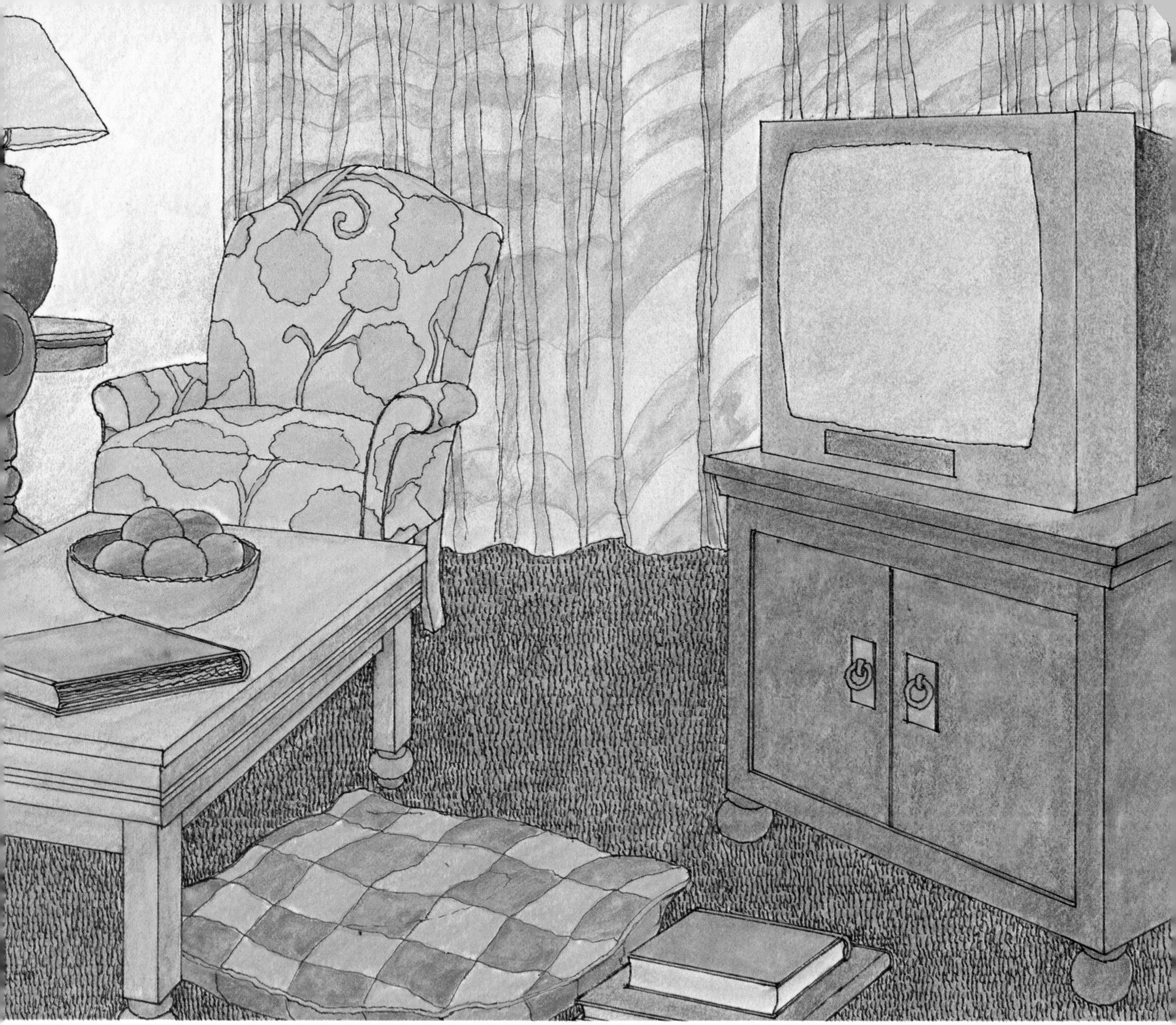

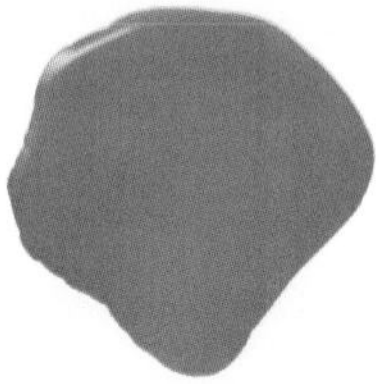

green

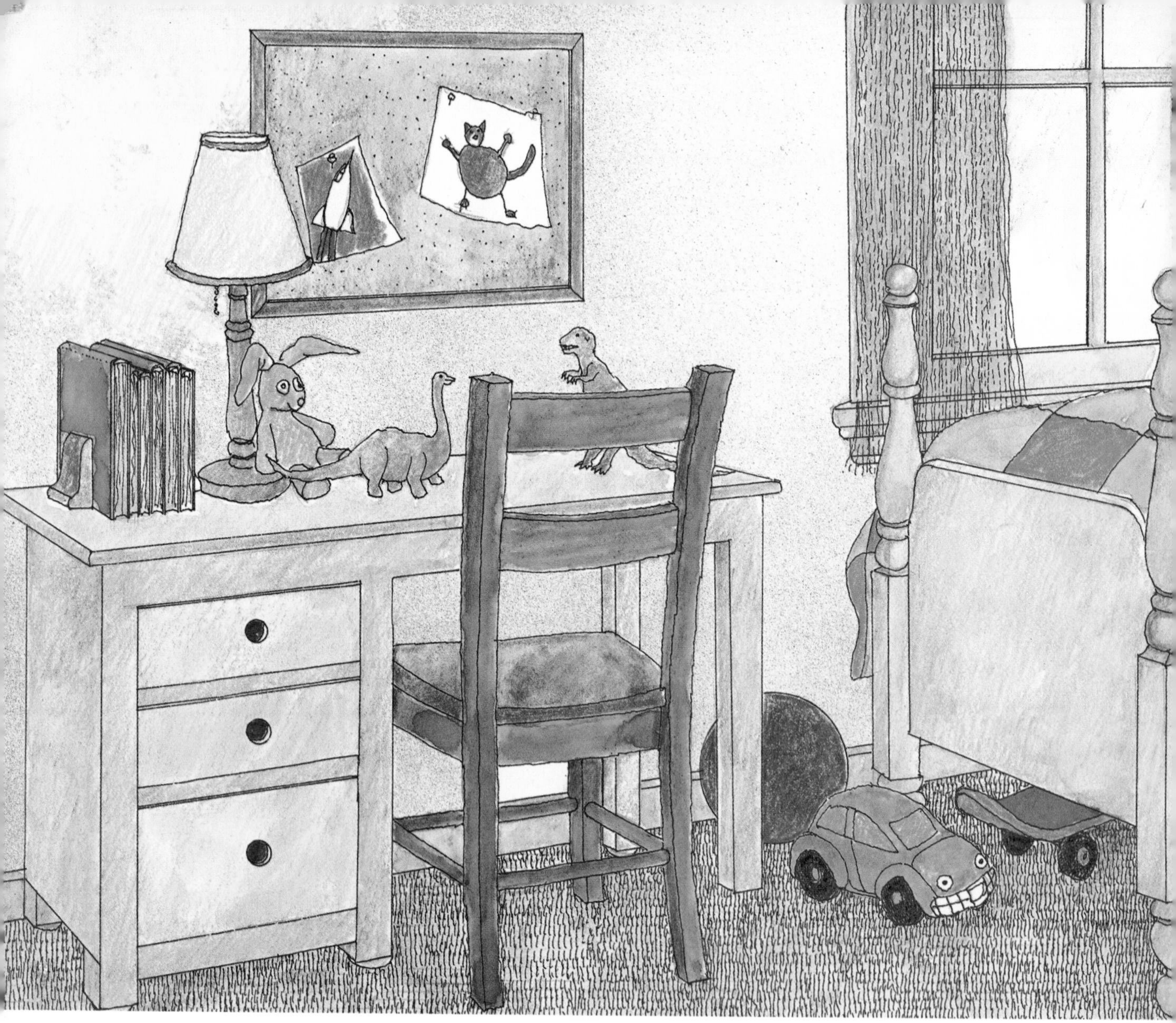

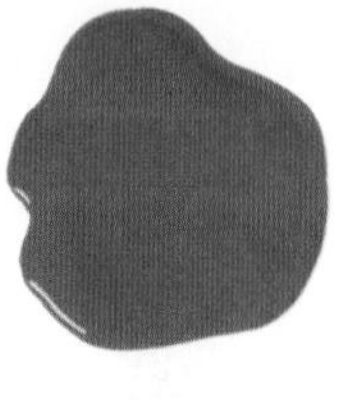

orange

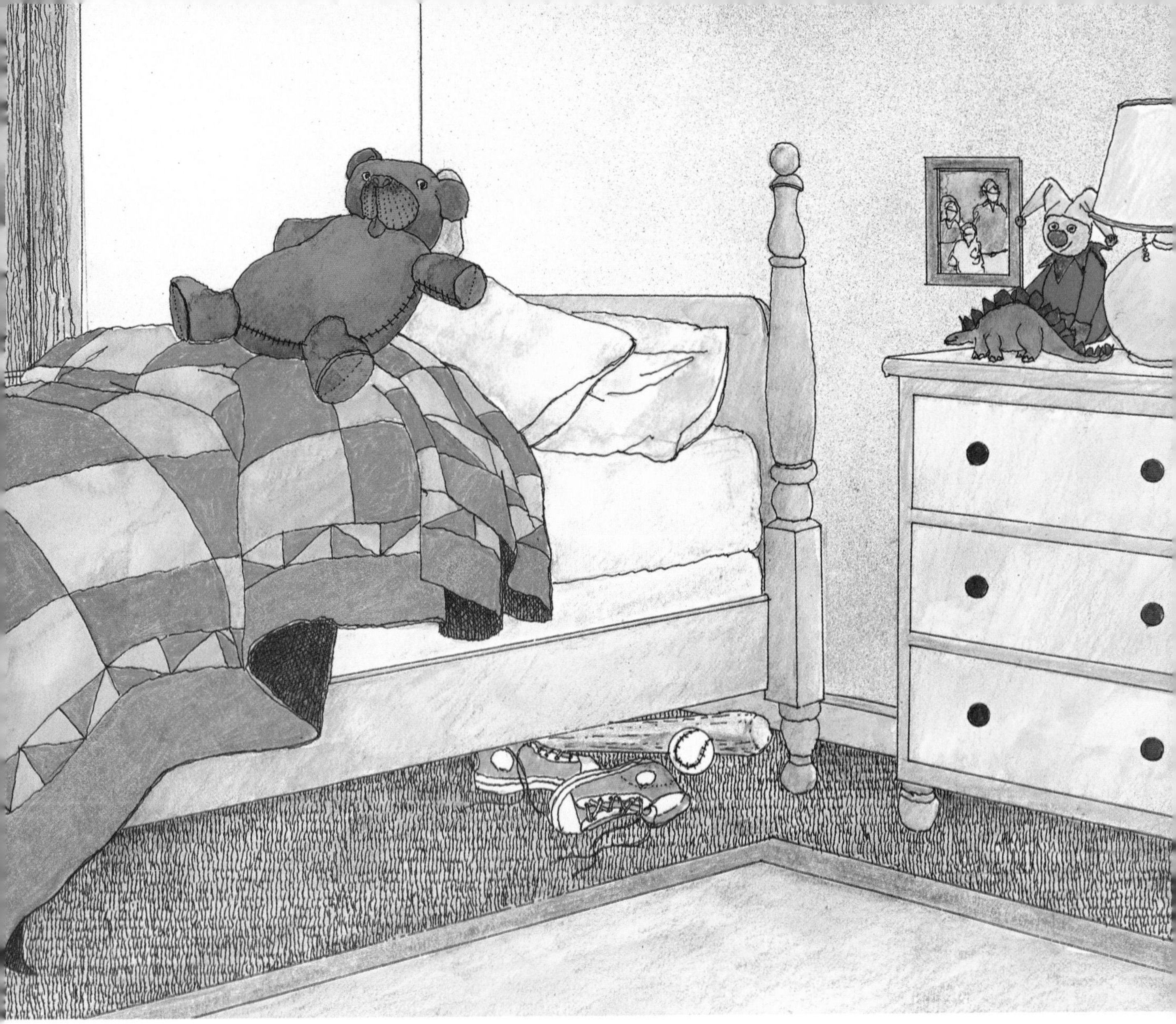

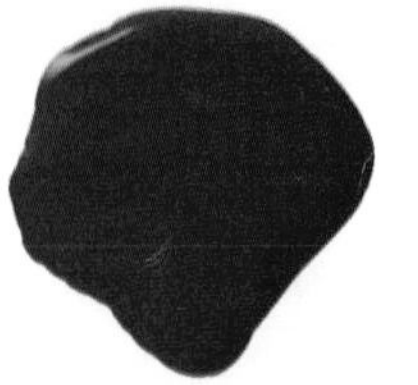

purple

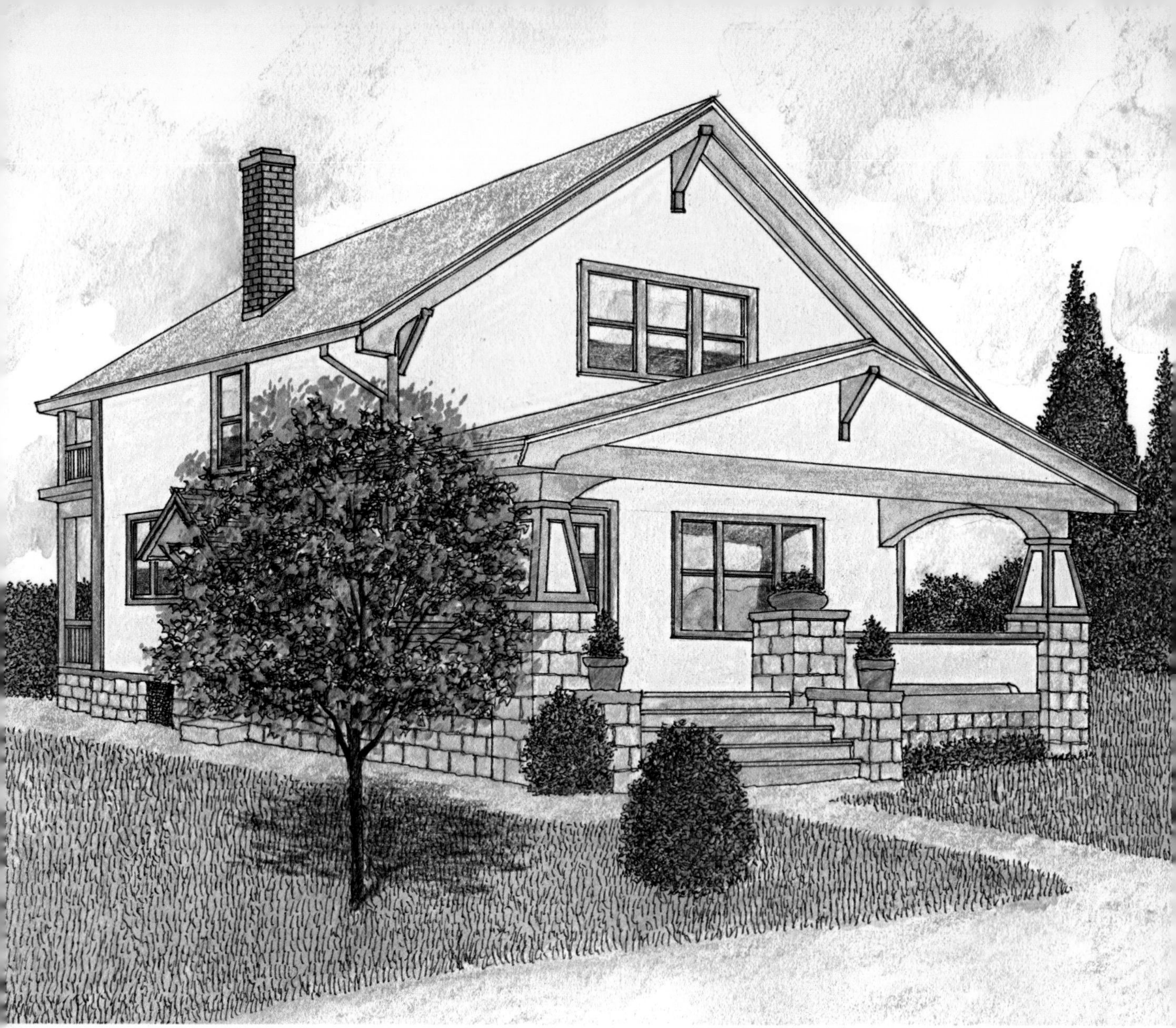

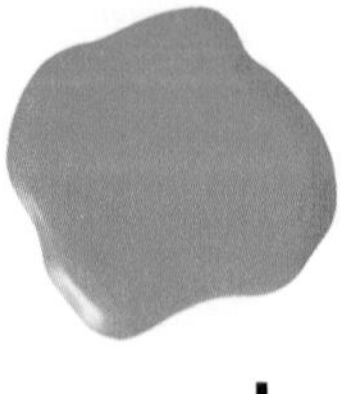

pink